Prodigal

Prodigal

Michael C. Davis

Washington, DC

Copyright © 2019 Michael C. Davis

New Academia Publishing 2019

All rights reserved. No part of this book may be reproduced or transmitted in any form or by any means, electronic or mechanical, including photocopying, recording, or by any information storage and retrieval system.

Printed in the United States of America

Library of Congress Control Number: 2019907444
ISBN 978-1-7326988-9-5 (alk. paper)

 An imprint of New Academia Publishing

New Academia Publishing
4401-A Connecticut Avenue NW #236, Washington DC 20008
info@newacademia.com - www.newacademia.com

Cover photo, "Trevor, Indian Ocean" by Mark C. Fox

For My Father

Contents

Acknowledgements ix

Annunciation	1
Opening a Book	2
Salidas	3
Off the Boat	5
Cleaning the Catch	6
Drawing the Flame	7
Hallgerd's Husband	8
Hunger	10
The Lover Should Not Have Returned	12
The Prodigal	13
Serenata	14
The Boy	16
Axes and Canoes	18
Shade-Tree Mechanics	19
Persian Miniature	20
Sunlight Reflecting Off Clouds	22
Into the Blue	23
Human Resources	27
Under the Streetlight	28
Scenes	29
Lies and Dreams	30
Pissing Her Name in the Snow	31
Loose Flesh	32
Depression	34
Specimen	35
No Turning Back	36
Telemachos	38
Summer, and the dead	41
Author's Biography	43

Acknowledgements

"Hallgerd's Husband" and "The Lover Should not Have Returned" were first published in *Poet Lore* and also appear in the chapbook, *Upon Waking*, Mica Press. "The Prodigal" was first published in *Upon Waking*. "Serenata" and "Persian Miniature" were first published in the journal, *Innisfree*. *No Turning Back* and *Salidas* were first read on Joe Gouveia's radio program Poets Corner, WOMR, Provincetown, MA. "Sunlight Reflecting Off Clouds" will appear in *Gargoyle*. "Last Moth of Autumn" was published by the Arlington County Moving Words competition.

I thank my friends-in-poetry, Patricia Garfinkel, Laura Brylawski-Miller, and Kathi Wolfe, for their comments and insight. And Grace Cavalieri for her advocacy.

Annunciation

A Rembrandt hangs in a room of the Hermitage, the size
of a wall. Abraham, sees angels passing, on the road,
invites them to his home. He seats the strangers
on the terrace, offers them refreshment. Sarah watches
from the doorway. The angels announce she will bear
a child. They are present among us, like ghosts
or the dead. The sun and moon turn silently
about the sky. Abraham's neighbors peer suspiciously
from windows, through hedges. Might the bright strangers
rise in their finery like itinerants and ask is there a verse
you'd particularly like to hear us read?
Abraham simply brings sweet cakes and wine.

Opening a Book

Its beauty is how it begins:
cover, endpapers, flypaper, title page,
copyright, and dedication
unnumbered but counted
as if they were inmates
sent into darkness
without processing,
untatooed.

The Roman numerals then start
their march as the pages of content,
acknowledgment, and foreword
making their strides
before the odd Arab 1, wāḥid,
leaves its invisible friend, zero,
behind

and the book begins
in earnest. Characters
and words, lined and orderly,
driven into the wet recesses
to the end we all face:
blood, synapse, vapor, smoke.

Salidas

The shoe was the sign
that it walked away by itself.
No one would own up to it.
What could she have done?

Or he? It was not his shoe.
He had not hidden it in his bag.
No plot lay behind
the disappearance. Yet,
the shoe was gone.

They shared a bed.
Somehow, the shoe
and the bed
were connected.

With the shoe skipping off
somewhere, the bed
somehow was broken.
It would no longer support
the both of them.

She had to announce
the disappearance in public.
The population had changed.
No one would own up to it.
No one would say, It was I.
I got home and saw that the shoe
would not fit. It must have been
the wine. I confess.

No one confessed.
The shoe skipped town.
The bed frame would no longer
hold. Eventually, locks
were changed. Bags were packed.
The phone stayed in its cradle.

He didn't really understand.
She missed the shoe.
How it could dance.
She missed him
and all that had gone before.
But she had to go.
So did he.

Certainly, someone
somewhere in darkness
must be laughing.

But the distance had grown
between them
and there was no way
to step back
because it hurt.

Off the Boat

Mother told me how Eleanor
    was locked twelve years in a tower
    and forgotten for spite.

600 years later the thin blood of her heirs
    rose to scratch a living
    delousing souls in highland Georgia.

Prospering little, they sank into the dry
    fields preaching to the unshod,
    the unlettered. One brother

Had his children cut willow switches and wait
    behind the house when the balance
    between sin and proper behavior needed adjustment.

The other took off for Texas looking for the real
    God—came back broken. Never spoke of it.
    Died crazy in a ditch.

Today, my father can't let go
    of the Romanov fortune he says his old man's
    old man was always talking of.

Great-grandfather Roman's given name
    is not even ours. It peels from our tongues
    like paper from an attic wall, letting the old show through.

Father's other side was just German. He had little
    to say of them. Their keepsake clippings lie now between
    pages of a lost blackletter natural history book, unread.

Cleaning the Catch

As a child attending to my father's love —
fishing — I refused to clean

the bass, pumpkin-ear, and bream we caught.
Killing the cold quivering flesh
made me squeamish, infinitely sad.

So he would sever the head
from behind the gills, then split
the belly and spill the guts.

Tail to absent head, I would drive the knife
like a razor, against the grain, scattering the salty
scales into the bright air.

When it came time for my mother to die,
ridden by cancer, she too quivered.
How I wanted her to stay.

And on that dock I find
one iridescent scale still clings.
Life lost, both wanted and wanting.

Drawing the Flame

Once, the darkness of an evening on any street
would be punctuated with the snap of a match,
the flick of a lighter, followed quickly by the cup

of a hand, a face briefly illuminated, the quick cast
of an eye. Then, with the flick of a wrist, the snap
of a thumb, darkness again.

Where are we now in this holy place, the streets
no longer peopled by those faithful mendicants,
rapt in flame, seeing to their momentary need?

Palms together they have passed into the wind,
their breath one sharp uptake,
a thin exhalation of smoke.

Hallgerd's Husband

Let us talk about that man who struck
his wife and then rowed with his servants
twenty-five miles out to his islands
to replenish wasted stores. While his men
staggered under loads of dried cod
he fidgeted a shuttle deep in his nets
knotting the black twine hard, cutting
his forefinger. His black blood set
in motion spotted the basalt shingle.
And while the bright bruise on Hallgerd's
cheek twisted before him, it also hung
before her father's eyes, who'd been told of the blow and followed.

Hearing another keel drag on the beach, the husband
is surprised, his fear betrayed only by his eyes.
The father stands confidently. The servants are over
the rise. A great-ax, bound in iron, rests
comfortably upon his shoulder.
The husband looks out at the hard green sea
behind his fish-veil and senses the inches
between his hand and sword, the moment
he has between the creation of the swell
and its crash on the beach. The father
glances from the gray strakes of the boat
to the line of the hill, the horizon's long, cold arc.

"Your marriage is bad," he says.
"Let me fix it." The husband sees the red
bruise again on his wife's white and willful
cheek. He reaches too late and unaware
of the tick and whir, the hammering steel
against bone, the gong in his heart pounding
fruitless an alarm. The father places
one last blow, cleaves the man from clavicle

to crotch, then smashes the servant's boat. He rows
back to his daughter. "I have freed you
to marry a second time," he will say to her
at the dock, his ax still bloody in the boat-ribs.

Hunger

The old heron in the river
takes one stitch a day,
one stitch ...
basting the water's edge
to the shade overhanging the bank.

Leg-deep in a seam
of hydrilla, he stands
over his piece of river
like a cloud, firmly planted,
his prey lured into shelter.

Everything is searching
and the night will be long.

A quick stab
in the water
and he is fed.

Late at dusk
he flies,
almost without work,
each wingbeat sure,
over the loose fabric
of homes knit
shoulder to shoulder

where we sleep
as close together
as our hunger
will allow.

Over us all
he coils,
a single letter
without a word.

The Lover Should Not Have Returned

We tearme sleep a death, and yet it is waking that kills us, and destroys those spirits which are the house of life.
— Sir Thomas Browne

When I entered the apartment
and found you sitting in that exquisite
robe, a wedding band gleaming dimly
on the penultimate finger of your left
hand, forelengthened in the bedclothes,
I knew I had lost you. Sheets
of mud fell from my rotting shoes

and the hall loomed in the sheen
of your eyes like a reflection clinging to one
last ascending breath. There was nothing
behind them. Your right hand cupped
a breast as simply as if it were
the knob to a door that you might open
or close, and below that hand our whippet lay

asleep, or waiting to lunge, I could
no longer tell. Her thin, hairless tail
curled beneath a flank. From behind her slitted
lids she stared as if to guard a tomb,
so still she might have been cut from stone
the moment before — she made no move to leap
in greeting or rub in my old spell.

I leaned and whispered in your ear, be sure
to bury your dead deep, or they'll rise
like the drowned to poke their moldering snouts
from beneath the skirts of lilies.
You covered your breast with dark
silk. I turned to the door, unheard. My footprints
backed out, trailing earth to the fields.

The Prodigal

Each sound from the carnival slips
over the garden wall like a thief
after apricots in the bower
where now he rests, remembering his ladies'
kisses, and the taste of the wine.

At the door, on the day of his return,
the servants smirked and his brother
hissed "old fool" at their father,
but only the prodigal heard.

The air is still. In the distance
a calliope pipes, calling him back
to the wheel. The rose in his hand
is just a dying flower on a dying stem.

Where is the world where things have not
been plucked or replanted? A servant
calls from the kitchen that the feast
of return is ready. The family will gather.

The son picks a yellow fruit dangling
 from an unpruned branch. The meal may cool.
His teeth plow a furrow to the pit.
The juice rises wildly behind his eyes.

Serenata

> *All nature is a commune of offering and taking, compassion and sacrifice.*
> — Gary Snyder

Play
for me
as if youth was long, this night
forever, death distant,
and the guttering flame
beyond fluttering to nothing,
a moth's wing.

Cradle
the guitar
and touch its neck, belly
for a note — robust and pure —
to face darkness without
flinching. Play as if the small
bones that make your hands
were spirited away
and only the tune
remained to speak
of what fine things they once were.

One day
cataclysm will come.
The angels will open their phials
and crack the graves.
There will I lie stripped —
skull askew, the bones
of my spine, girdle, and legs
resounding in their eyes
like a fork to tune the air.

'Til then,
each note
departs the wood's polished curve
and makes its way against
the dark for at least
a while before it dies.
Blood loops through the fingers
for another turn. The earth
listens, still.

The Boy

In a distant city
a man
who has reached the end
of caring
wraps his boy
in a sheet
and goes about his day.

From when the moon
was new
to when the moon
was full
he has left the boy,
his damaged boy,
wrapped in a sheet,
and gone about the business
of his day.

The father
has reached the end.
His boy so sick
he cannot eat
or wash, or dress,
or move. But it is his
boy, carefully tucked
in a sheet.

The boy has starved,
but not for love.
The boy who the father
could no longer wash,
or dress, or move,
or feed.

In a bed
to which the father
returns, the boy lies.
His boy still to sleep
beside, after the end
of the business of the day.

The boy,
unseeing, agape,
lies beside his father.

It is his boy.
The father cradles him,
alone, in the city
at the end of caring.

Axes and Canoes

When I am troubled by what is on the news
the wasted children, falling bombs, and fire,
I'm certain all the future will require is axes and canoes.

Chips fly from the blade that hews
a white smile deep in the trunk. My arms don't tire
when I am troubled by what is on the news.

The out-of-kilter tree's leaves and hues
rattle against the sky, then fall against my ire.
I'm certain all the future will require is axes and canoes.

Hollowed and hardened with fire, I'll use
the downed tree as a vessel. Water beckons, bright as wire,
when I am troubled by what is on the news.

The flash of paddle, the lapping wake amuse.
The slap of wave on hollow hull sounds sweeter than a choir.
I'm certain all the future will require is axes and canoes.

The king of Babylon once dreamed a great tree was abused
then ran mad as a beast through forest, his city put to fire.
When I am troubled by what is on the news,
I'm certain all the future will require is axes and canoes.

Shade-Tree Mechanics

Everything that has been made
can be disassembled. The switch,
clutch, transistor, flower, even
the arm, the hand, the head.

The trick, always, is getting it back
together again. This morning I stand
covered in grease to the left of my car
with the transmission in my hands,

ready for work: pulling and replacing
seals, cleaning shafts, loosening
and then retightening
bolts to the correct torque.

How different am I from the doctor
who removed my wife's breast,
closed her neatly,
forgot nothing inside?

The transmission will go back
with a little force, finesse —
the reverse of removal, the book says.

Over her ribs
I can trace the raw scar,
the pale field of a graft.

My beautiful tools glisten,
laid out like surgeon's knives
on pale red mechanic's cloth.

Each removal, repair, renewal,
has its recommended technique.
But not a wrench in the world
reverses the inexorable wear.

Persian Miniature

Timur sits on two rugs,
one only partially unrolled,
apart from his retinue.

His wine-bearers are frozen
in gestures of offering.

Across a small creek
whose voice will mingle
with other melodies
musicians sit
and pluck harp,
tap tambourine.

Fire of battle
still smolders
in the exalted one's eyes.
An orange tree
behind him
offers untaken shade.

The great city of India
lies at his feet,
taken.
There is no parade.

A simple shift
covers his back.
Violets embroider
the grass
carpeting
the hillside.

The music
is not heard,
nor the voice
of the brook.
The field lies ready
for the scythe.

Sunlight Reflecting Off Clouds

No, it is off the face of Olympus. The wood below.
The mirror lake. The stones stacked in remembrance,
the light off the sea as the waves curl toward some mythic beach
where Thetis and Peleus couple. The war will not be
a good one for the child. First, she tempers him slowly over fire.
Later she cools him in the river separating the living
from the dead. She educates him with the best teacher,
a were-horse—steeped in instinct and knowledge.
But the empty sky offers no protection.
Desperate, she schools him as a girl. But when offered by the Greeks,
he chooses the sword. Let the linens go. Someone
else will embroider the skirt, the tale, the winding sheet.
And when it comes time, the chattering gods,
the king's counsel, his brothers-in-arms, the screaming
tube of collapsed air that is his fate, will sing to him.
As other blood pours from the city, he hears the voice of his mother,
the voice of the daughter of wind and sea,
whetted, keen, and high. What she could not help
but let him know: the old murthering lullaby.

Into the Blue

> *Porter, take your basket and follow me.*
> — Alf Layla wa Layla

I

There are those days
that follow the pattern
of all days,

where like the boy
in some tale you gaze
at the back of the stove

from your warm spot
and there is little need
to move.

And there are those days
that start out
as all others

but somewhere
after a deal is cut
and the price is named

the haze is stripped
from what will become
and some other path is taken.

One path is to go
the way of the Porter
in the Thousand and One

Nights: hired by a woman
to go to the grocer,
the florist, nut vendor, butcher,

baker, and perfume stall
before bearing the load to her house
where now with two sisters

she jokes that a fourth leg is needed
to support the table
of the world.

Harun al Rashid
disguised, connives
his way through the door

to sit among you.
The women within the privacy
of their home

strip and play.
Plucked instruments, a tambourine,
sound from behind a screen.

Kissed, caressed, and aroused,
the sisters enter a pool. Three one-eyed
dervishes arrive, and you all are told,

under the threat of death,
you cannot question
what is to occur.

Before your eyes
a dog is flogged
and the mark of the whip

appears on the pale skin
of one naked girl.
You cry out,

are bound, threatened,
forgiven, and caught again
in another tale

from which there is no escape.
The world is no longer
what it seems.

You cannot return
to what it was.

II

And there are other paths,
too, that begin
as mundanely as any other.

You take the 6
downtown at six-thirty,
climb to the street,

cross the plaza,
pass the church,
enter the lobby,

board the elevator,
and rise to the day's labor.
It is only after you see

the jet enters the floor below
and feel the building move
beneath your feet,

that you notice,
in the billowing smoke,
among the shattered struts of heaven,

an angel with broken wings
beckoning to the only way out.
Between what we have made

of earth, and the light
fluttering in the sky,
you face a story

forever changed.
Morning has overtaken Shahrazade.
She lapses into silence.

Ink,
like blood,
flows onto the page.

Blood,
like speech,
evaporates.

You cannot return
to what you were.

Human Resources

A tired voice mumbles, "brutal alarm." But the ring
is only insistent. On my side, I think of an alarm
more fitting. A call to arms, the defense of the state.
Katyn, Smolensk. Spring 1940. Stalin's executioner
prepares for his day. Waking, dressing, gathering
the Walther. Slipping on the glove to defend
the palm against recoil. Lacing the butcher's apron.
Entering the soundproof bunker like a figure in a clock
on a square in some old European town. The opening
door, the kneeling body, the damning papers. The charge,
discharge, and off to the wood.
Another bullet, a ditch already waiting.

In London, the free Poles plead to intervene,
to descend from the miserable sky where
they are held, and uncover the atrocity. Their request
is bound in red, tied with a ribbon, available at last,
half a century later in a box on a shelf in the Diplomatic
Branch of the National Archives: General File,
Diplomatic and Military Relations
of the United States: Poland 1939-44.

Under the Streetlight

Last moth of autumn,
feathery and golden as the now-turned oak,
with wings that brush the wind
as gently as a closing lash
against a cheek,
whose pheromone
do you seek,
on this damp and lonely night?

We both turn ragged
beneath this false moon
without promise of increase.

Scenes

I

A mother tells her child she tried twice,
without success. The oven
door dropped like a jaw. The pilot
flame blown out. Her head in.
Before her parents returned.

II

Over dinner, a father confesses
his wife's cancer death really was suicide.
The bitter gas failed.
Chemo's rejection succeeded.

III

A child walks down a hall. A thousand
doors. Faucets drip, dogs bark,
vertical blinds blow onto balconies.
A final opening to the incinerator.
Blue sky above. Untucked mortar between
blackened brick, to the bottom.
Where truth may lie.

Lies and Dreams

I've got a bag of figs
I've got a sty
that's full of pigs
with curly tails
and shoveling noses
and all around
it's covered in roses
I've got a bag of figs.

I've got a jar of lies
and a cake on the counter
covered in flies
with buzzing wings
they lay their eggs
their hairy tongues feast
on the sweetening dregs
I've got a jar of lies.

You had a pocket of dreams
'til you emptied it out
in one of those streams
that flows to the sea
as quick as can be
without a thought
you let it out
you had a pocket of dreams.

We have a problem it seems
with my lies and pigs
and your let-go dreams
the house with a cake
on the counter in crumbs
and the roses climbing
and twisting their thumbs
we have a problem it seems.

Pissing Her Name in the Snow

Sometimes the urge to write is so strong
any surface will do. So the lover thinks
one snowy eve stumbling home from a pub,
the urge to go so strong. And what else is

such a thin coverlet if not a blank
page begging for an inscription? It was
after all three drops of blood burned
in the snow that focused Parsifal

on his pressing quest and the absence
of his wife. So the lover recalls. The motions
necessary to write with such a soft pen
are akin to those needed to navigate

a crowded floor with two brimming pints—
a little lead, a feint, a thrust. Golden cursive
steams darkly on the whiteness. Finished,
he thinks there you have it, zipping himself up.

Loose Flesh

It cannot be gathered,
this meat,
the straying middle
of men.
Belts only cinch it.
There are
waistbands to hike
over it,
but in the end
they are
of no help.

Loose it is
there
leaning against the lamppost,
waiting for the train
in the tired
once-black shoes
repaired thrice
that have flattened
into dark puddles
that fortunately
do not reflect.

"Who am I?" the man
asks the blind eye
at the peak of the mountain
he has become.
"I am not feeling myself
anymore."
The wandering pile
slides south
with gravity's help,
its desire
buried,
straddled,
thwarted.

He dreams
he will stand
at the end of some
road north, like the hero
he still imagines,
an oar over his shoulder
ready to build
at last,
to begin.

But in the thick
middle of his gut
an artery
beats time.
The hour has arrived,
the train enters.
"Go on," the mountain
of flesh says to itself.

Entering, he looks
askance
at the faces turning
toward him.
Willing
and unwilling
to move he listens
for the roar of the chain,
the anchor's certain fall.

Depression

My father
the retired military engineer
sits in a chair
not his own
reading a mystery
whose name he will not reveal.

I'm reading trash,
he says.
He is not proud.
Every trip out the door
is a blow; every visit
an assault.

At half past eight
and half past five
he takes his meals.
Without help,
he has not walked in the wind
in four years.

Why see a film,
he asks. I saw one
once. The book he reads
he reads
again and again.

Specimen

He is 90, demented, bipolar, depressed, incontinent.
A doctor wants a urine sample. I walk him
to the bathroom, close the door. Unbuckle the belt.
Unzip the fly. Drop the diaper. He doesn't connect
the open commode, the cup, the bladder, the need.
Even when I hold him. The body he no longer knows
he has.

No Turning Back

The doctor worries.
He is no longer an infant.

He needs surgery for a large
stone in his bladder. She orders
an echocardiogram

followed by a stress test.
On Tuesday a technician smears
his old bared torso

with acoustic gel
and applies the wand. He lies
on an examining table.

I sit on a chair.
The tech searches.
I watch the screen.

His heart appears, a sectioned
geode at the center
of his earth.

The technician
switches on the sound
and we are awash

in gurgles of outflow.
The valve snaps to,
the ventricle contracts.

His heart marches
as a troop across the parade ground
at West Point, years ago

before the war. As it has marched
now, into its 87th year.
Through the ranks,

marriage, children,
retirement, mania,
separation, dementia.

The drum still beats
within him.
His classmates

drop on the sidelines.
In the tangled wood
his life has become

black ravens feast
on the crusts he dropped.
The valve snaps to.

The ventricle contracts.

Telemachos

> Οὖτις ἐμοί γ' ὄνομα (No man is my name) — *Odyssey*, 9.366

The poet I dream
who tells my father's story
never gets the facts right.

Blindly he imagines
Odysseus only 20 years gone,

young when he left,
commanding when he returned,
strengthened by his journey,
at ease with his gods.

Instead,
I find him
30 years out
dim-eyed, toothless,
no muscle
on his bones,
his wife dead,
house ransacked,
bow unstrung.
Broken.

He brings back
only a faint taste
of the sea
and a smell
on his breath
of decay,
babbling about ruin,
women who were not wives,
a trip to Hades,
and loss
how everything has been
lost.

Oh,
he is happy to see me,
If he could only remember my name,
firstborn,
fruit of a tree
that can no longer hold
the twittering remains
of our family
in its Ithacan branches,
long since chopped
and burned.

I watch him pick
flotsam
from the beach.
Net floats,
driftwood,
broken oars —
piling them onto his pitiful
offering to Poseidon.

The poet I dream
will have Odysseus
launch his ship
again, and reserves for him
a special place in Hell.

They do that,
dreamers.
I should know.

But the part
of the son who waited
for his father's
return will have
no such fame.

I have lingered too long
In the dry hills
of middle age
for the return of no man,
and find myself now
fully rewarded.

Summer,
and the dead

mow their lawns
in the neighborhood
each evening.

They cannot leave,
they have lived here
so long.

Fallen in the shower,
shot through the heart
by their own hand,
autumn's leaves
fall through them
as they drop,
fluttering
and unhearing.

Winter is too quiet.

In the spring,
we all rise
dreaming and triumphant.
We launch our mowers
against the green tide.
Light our barbeques,
the fuse sparkles
into summer,
a season
of dogs resurrected
from old flowerbeds
long since mowed over.
The former owners
of our homes
walk the dogs

on dirt lanes
now paved
and stop to speak
of the change
below the rising voices
of dog-day cicadas,
beneath the darkening shade
of maple, oak, walnut, tulip.

Again, we tire,
the dead and us.
Summer's green, dusky,
and its sky, blue
and implacable.

Those of us alive
wish for rest.
And those at rest
press on
turning each stick
and stone
under the gently
wheeling stars,
asking no more
of those at the end
of their leads
who must follow.

Author's Biography

Photo by Alexandra Russell

Michael Davis's chapbook, *Upon Waking*, Mica Press was published in 1999. His work has appeared in *Poet Lore, Lip Service, Innisfree, Minimus, Gargoyle,* and the anthologies *Open Door, Cabin Fever,* and *Winners*. He has read extensively in the Washington, D.C., area and has participated for two decades in the Arlington County Pick-a-Poet program, teaching poetry in county schools.

www.ingramcontent.com/pod-product-compliance
Lightning Source LLC
Chambersburg PA
CBHW031206160426
43193CB00008B/530